CREATURES IN COUTURE

To all the little creatures,
running up with a book in hand,
I can't wait to read this with you.

-D.K.

Diana Kohan-Ghadosh Hamadani is a Los Angeles based illustrator, designer and creature.
This is her debut picture book.

Author's notes and recommendations:

Make a lot of exaggerated facial expressions while pronouncing the words.
Use your arms to express yourself, maybe even your shoulders. Channel the creature.
This behavior may result in giggles.

No animals were harmed during the couture fittings, which all took place in my imagination.

Printed and bound in USA by Ingramspark
ISBN: 979-8-218-36939-2 (Print / Softcover)
ISBN: 979-8-218-39619-0 (Print / Hardcover)
Ebook Available

CREATURES IN COUTURE

Written & Illustrated By

Diana Kohan-Ghadosh

A
Armadillos Wear Azzedine ALAïA

Butterflies
Wear
Wear
B
BALMAIN

Cockatoos
wear
COCO
CHANEL

Deers Wear CHRISTIAN DIOR

Elephants wear
ERDEM

Flamingos Wear FENDI

Goats
wear
Gucci

H
Hedgehogs Wear Hermes

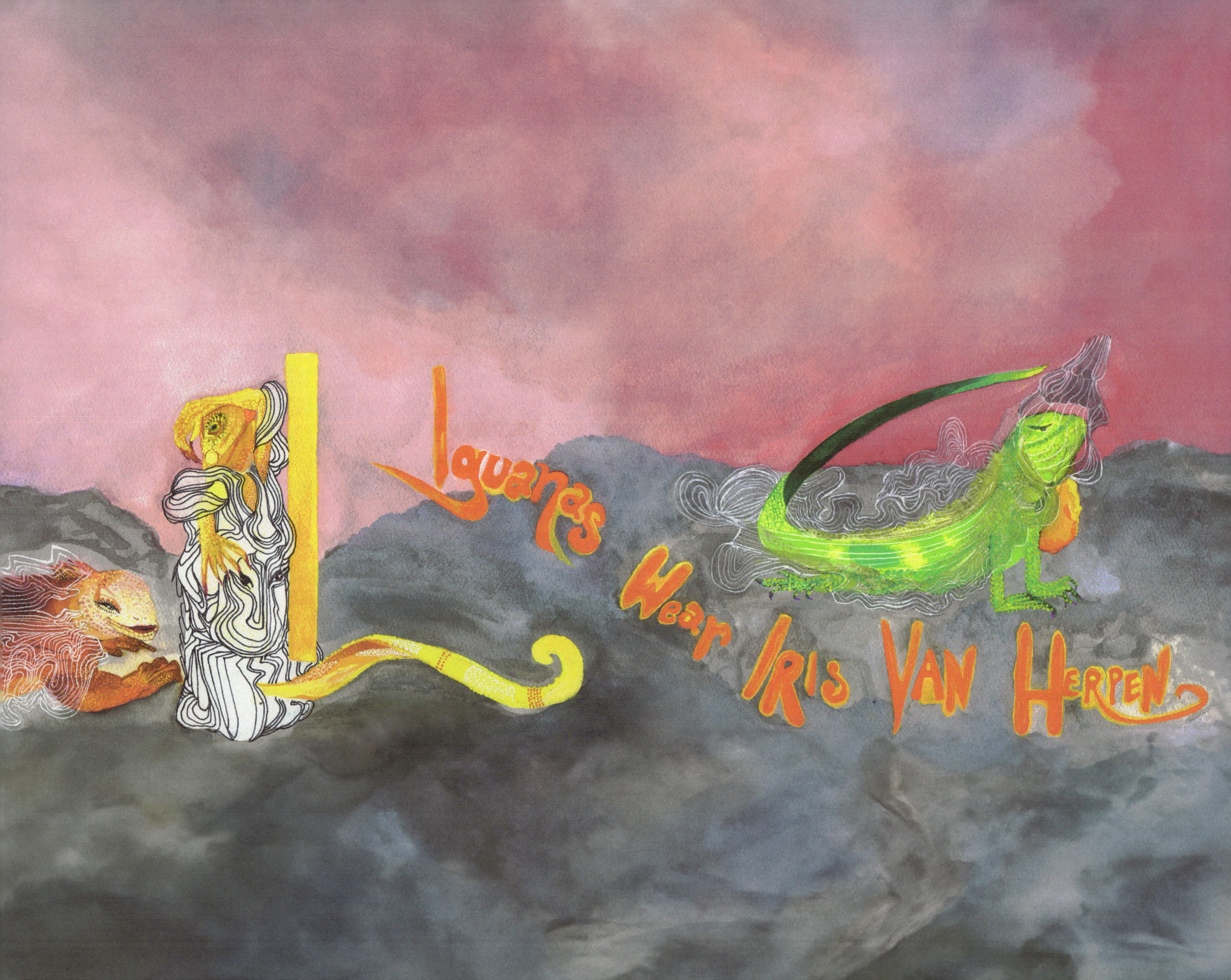

Iguanas Wear Iris Van Herpen

J
Jaguars wear JACQUEMUS
Jaguars

Koalas wear Kenzo

Llamas Wear
Louis Vuitton

Monkeys Wear
M
Maison Martin
Margiela

N
Newts Wear
Naeem Khan

Octopuses
Wear
OFF-WHITE

P
Penguins wear PRADA

Quails Wear Alexander McQueen
Q

Rabbits Wear Rodarte

Swans Wear Schiaparelli

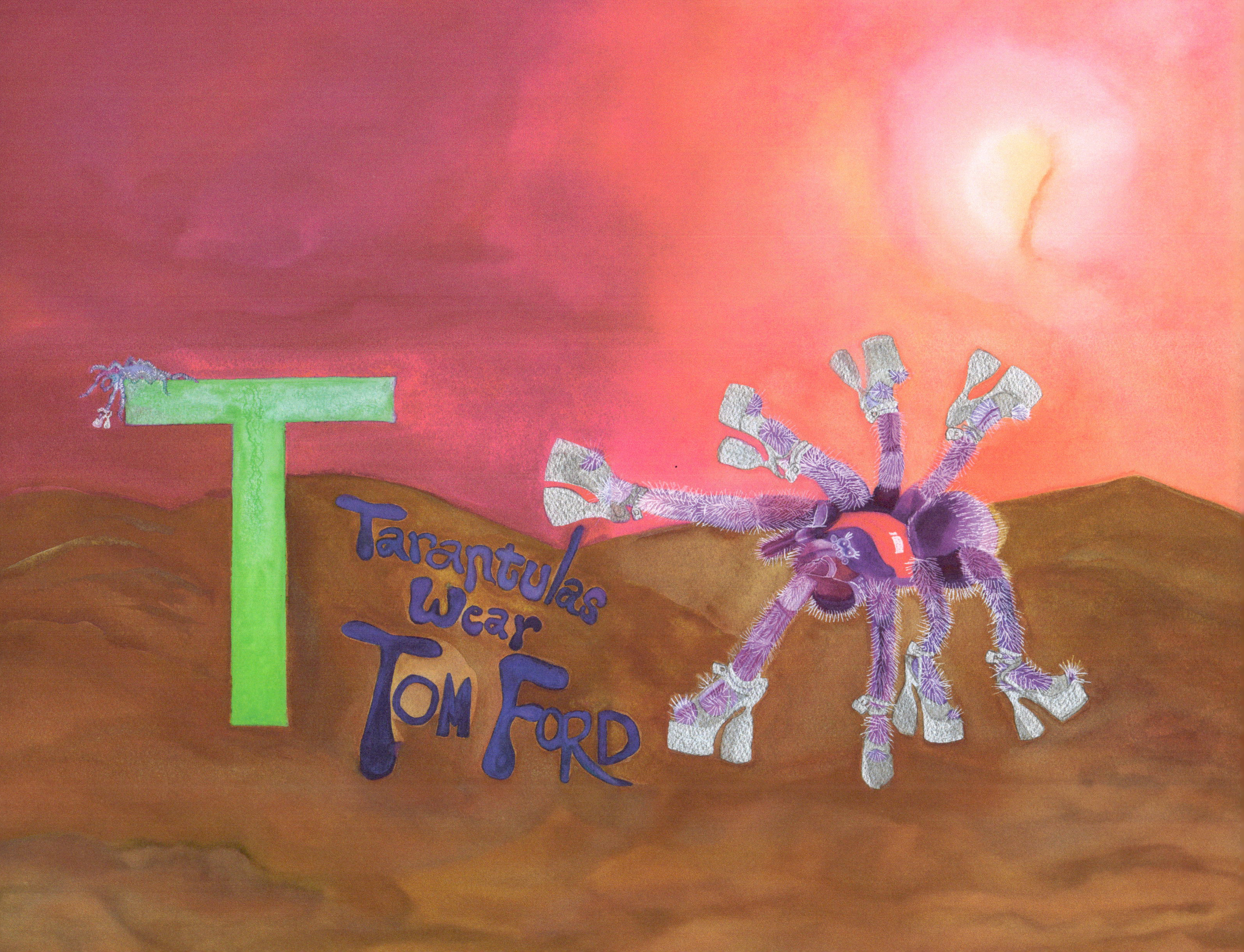

Tarantulas
Wear
Tom Ford

Unicorns wear EMANUEL
UWEAR

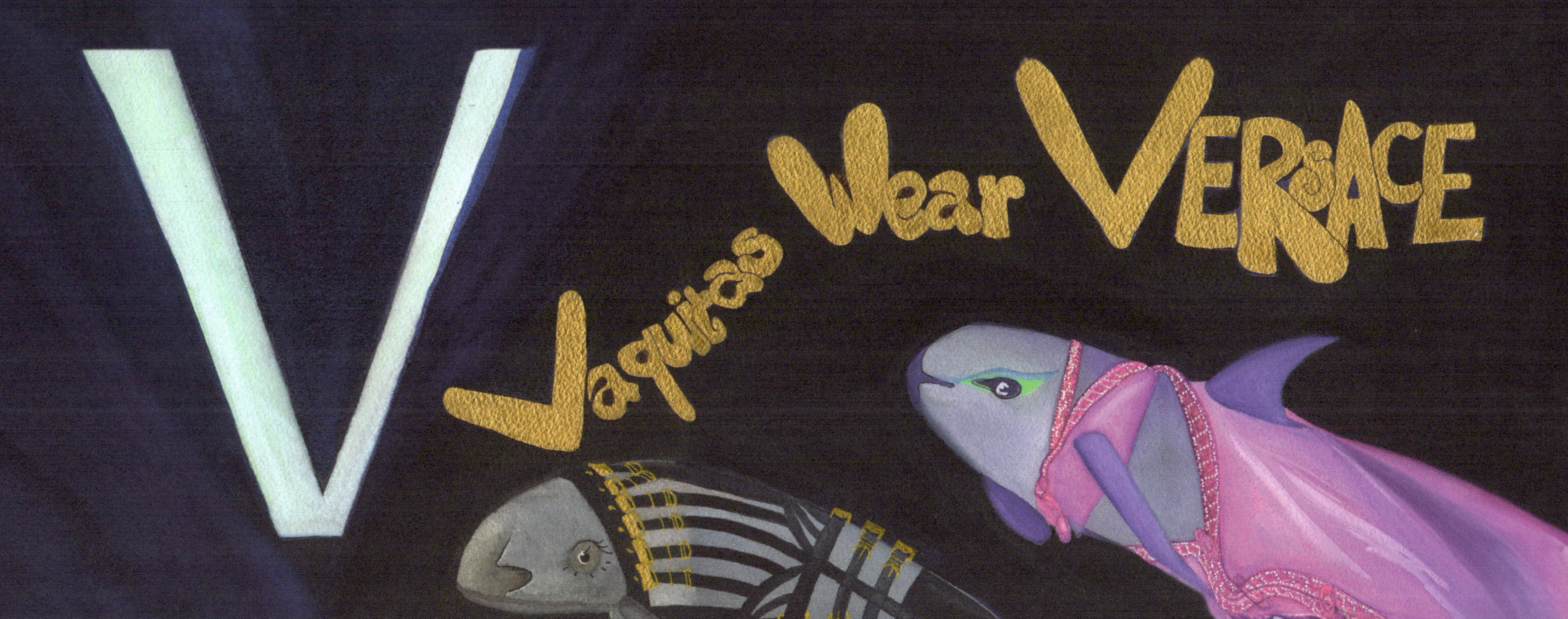
V
Vaquitas Wear VERSACE

W
WalruseS Wear WOLFORD

Xeruses Wear
XIMON LEE

Yaks Wear Yves Saint Laurent

Zebras Wear ZAC POSEN